SELECTED POEMS

of

MARIA LUISE WEISSMANN

translated by

William Ruleman

Published by Cedar Springs Books, 2015.

ISBN-13: 978-0692479681

ISBN-10: 0692479686

Acknowledgments

I am first of all grateful to the editors of the following journals, in which several of the poems in this book first appeared:

AALITRA Review for "The Gorilla," "Robinson Finds Himself on the Island Beach," "Just Open," "The Youth of a Prophet," "The Procession of the Animals," "An Evening in Early Autumn," and "Ancient"

The Eunoia Review for "Childhood" and "To My Father"

The Galway Review for "Robinson Finds Friday," "Don Quixote Struggles with God," and "On a Packet of Letters"

Poetry Salzburg Review for "The Hermit" and "Snow"

The Sonnet Scroll for "The Strange City," "Journeys," and "Sonnet"

I am also grateful to Ms. Trudy Miller, who graciously listened as I read to her from Weissmann's originals and read my translations, offering suggestions for their revision in places; to the Appalachian College Association, for awarding me a summer fellowship to complete this book; to Dr. Brigid Maher of Latrobe University for writing on my behalf; to Dr. Suzanne Hine, Vice-President for Academic Affairs at Tennessee Wesleyan College, and my wife, Dr. Elizabeth Sayle Ruleman, Professor of English, Chair of English and Foreign Languages and Associate Dean of Humanities at Tennessee Wesleyan College, both of whom encouraged me to apply for the grant; and to the staff at the Monacensia Archive and the Münchner Stadtbibliothek (Munich City Library), who assisted me in my research on Weissmann's life and work.

TABLE OF CONTENTS

from *Imago*

FOREWORD

When the Munich-based poet Maria Luise Weissmann died unexpectedly of heart failure at the age of thirty, her literary contemporaries regarded her premature death a great tragedy, agreeing that the world had lost a poet of great promise and genius, one whose passing caused even as much grief as the recent death of Hugo von Hofmannsthal (Heuschel XII). Already, within the space of ten years, she had produced an auspicious first collection (*Das Frühe Fest*), a profound sequence of sonnet-like reflections on the title character of Daniel Defoe's *Robinson Crusoe*, a shorter sequence of *Dingedichte* in the manner of Rilke (*Mit einer kleinen Sammlung von Kakteen*), a not-yet-published book of new verse to be titled *Imago*, as well as the fragment of a novella, essays on figures such as Bettina von Arnim, Johann Wolfgang von Goethe, Rainer Maria Rilke, Gustav Meyrink, and Rudolf Alexander Schroeder, and translations of such French poets as Blaise Cendrars, Paul Verlaine, and Pierre Louys.

In 1932, Weissmann's husband, the publisher and writer Heinrich F. S. Bachmair, brought out *Gesammelte Dichtungen*, which featured, posthumously, all of her mature poetry, prose, and translations. In 1946, under the sanction of U. S. Military Information Control, he also printed an edition of her selected poems, to which he gave the name *Imago*, honoring his deceased wife's request as to the title of what she hoped would be her next volume.

Since then, various websites in German have posted her work online; and in 2013, Michael Holzinger of Berlin published a print edition of her poems and prose that resembles the 1932 edition in terms of what it features. However, up until now, no collection of her poems in English translation has appeared, so this edition is an attempt to bring Weissmann's work to the attention of an English-speaking audience and thus to help give it the wider readership that it deserves. Those seeking to explore Weissmann's poetry further, and in the original, should find the Holzinger edition to be a highly helpful and readily-available counterpart to this volume.

A NOTE ON THE TRANSLATION, AND ON
TRANSLATION IN GENERAL

Naturally, in my translations here, I have struggled to capture both the sound and sense of Weissmann's poetry, and adhering to her own meters and rhyme schemes seemed the most direct way of doing so. Still, those who come to this volume expecting renderings exact in every respect will be disappointed. To be sure, in every act of translation (and in the creation of any work of art, for that matter), regard for the *trinity of mind, body, and spirit* in a work is essential. Yet a balance—for the sake of *the unity of the whole*—must be struck among these three entities; and at times, though as seldom as possible, sacrifices must be made.

So I have departed from a strictly literal transcription at times to convey, with what grace I could, the general gist and spirit of Weissmann's poems in her own chosen forms. At times I have found myself engaging in the kind of wordplay that English affords but that finds no immediate equivalent in German. Yet I have done this to emulate, in my own tongue, Weissmann's own often playful tone. The result of such an endeavor will never, of course, be *the same* as the original. It is a *new poem*—a child, if you will, brought into the world from the wedding of two parents—a wholly new being who takes on the characteristics—mind, body, and spirit—of its forebears while also being its own original self.

I would like to say that any translator worth his or her salt will not do damage to a poem by approaching it in a strictly literal and analytical fashion, though I must concede that there is indeed the kind of translator who sees the original poem in the way that he or she would view an archeological find—as hieroglyphics to be deciphered, or as a mummy to be preserved, in a purely cold and detached and clinical way. This method results in the type of translation that inhabits a kind of arid no man's land between two tongues—the type that insists on strictly scholarly accuracy, even at the "expense of spirit" and feeling. True, this type can certainly act as a crib for those seeking to achieve a more or less pedestrian knowledge of another language, or even as an aid those whose knowledge of a language is rusty. Yet it can hardly claim to represent a poem's true music, soul, and meaning. Indeed, I tend to hold with Willis Barnstone that "songless translations mislead the reader, and this is not good scholarship, not close and not truly literal" (96).

Every great poem is a *living thing*, an organism, and will remain so despite the method by which is rendered into another tongue. Yet a translation that works as a poem in itself can give the original poem even greater life—by expanding the audience for it, by enlarging the ways it can be enjoyed, by enriching the aesthetic experience it affords.

Granted, anyone who approaches the act of translating in a reverent way, no matter what his or her theoretical bias may be, does so with the intent of doing the original poem justice. And if the translator puts all his or her heart, mind, and soul into the effort, there will always be his or her own imprint—physical and psychic as well as cerebral. The poem itself will remain intact: immortal. But earnest and soulful and carefully-crafted renderings will serve to illuminate a poem's greatness.

from DAS FRÜHE FEST (1918-22)

CHILDHOOD

A cut-glass cube lit up and filled the room
When evening came. He often held it fast
To bask in the dew-like glimmer of its bloom.
Dark birds outside would soar and flutter past,
Their flight a vast and chill and swirling sea
About his brow. At times he felt the rare
And strange songs round him cease—miraculously—
And sensed a flower singing in his hair.
Quite often, stooped by some vague weight, he'd creep
Along and deem himself a fire grown dim.
Eyes were agony for him, his hate for them deep;
The strange woods called yet also threatened him:
In darkness, stark white sticks of stags would stand,
Prepared to bear him off . . . Yet one bough raised,
In angry strokes, its crooked hand.

THE STRANGE CITY

The sky's been built quite close, with much cement,
Whitewashed all over with those gaudy blues
That advertising artists like to use.
Fate lurks in dark nooks: brooding, indolent.

And corners stare with fatalistic bent,
Then cliffs! I'm heaved against them suddenly
Until the flood (onrushing) crushes me.
I've lived through nights of autos' shrill lament;

All hope for lasting grace seems long since past.
Angelic voices, harp-strings' radiant sound,
O breath of prayers, palm scents . . . O wings' sweep!

I shove myself at gates rammed shut, locked fast;
I stare at myriad masks of fright all round;
I'm tired—so tired—yet cannot go to sleep.

JUNE 1919

The dark dawn bore me, heavy, in her womb
And for the pale morning, dying, brought me to be,
I who with the wild roses slowly bloom.
The hills must lend their cool blue shade to me
When midday hurts me with its sharp, steep glow.
The slim plank swaying over the brook below
Leads toward dusk with tired and timid tread.
The bare walls silently cave in at night;
The black woods stride their way about my bed.

THE GORILLA

Some time has passed since he breathed his sultry breeze,
Though his neck still bows with dreams of oceans. Then
He's in the sand once more, down on his knees,
Or sent right back to the iron bars again.
He'd gladly have, for his own, the parrot's blaze,
The scents of mignonettes, the waltz's sound;
Yet no beam breaks the glass of his eyes' dim glaze:
His hand bears the silent crease of his dream-dazed round
Past the strange lights silently, strangely slipping by.
At times, in his cry,
Which strikes from afar, he's wrenched into the Now
From the maw of sleep; and, erect as a monument,
He wrinkles the dome of his upturned brow
And strikes away at the stone-arched firmament.

CATS

They're very cool and pliable when they stride:
Their bodies flow along with gentle grace.
And when they spread their bloom-like paws out wide,
The earth receives their gait like an embrace.

Their look is humble and, at times, rather crazed;
And then their claws will spin, from silk and hair,
A strange and painfully-threaded mesh on dazed
And shattered shutters, cellar stair.

But in the evening, they're ecstatic, grand:
Enchanted nightly on their moon-white stones
And sick with longing, lust, and pain, they stand;
And all night long you hear their cries and moans.

LEVEL LANDSCAPE

Earth came, a grayish stream that gushed.
No dam could check her waters' pace.
Over mountain, vale, and house she rushed.
On the far horizon, the slim bright trace
Of a tree. Uprooted. Which falls into space.

THE CAROUSEL

They stood there deep in sleep, the beasts—so stiff
And mute and colorful and beautiful—
And listened to the same old jangling riff
Until a child's wince made them dutiful,

Alert. The lion's mane now flew anew,
Wind-tossed. The chime of bells commenced its song
From the elephant's teeth. The snout then snorted, drew
The proud caravan along in its threading throng,

On and on. Before its sharp departure lay
A forest of palms, enmeshed in some wild spree;
From deep in rockets shot the heated day;
Cacti burned in crimson immensity.

JOURNEYS

All day long I have to search for you,
And what surrounds you holds much hope for me.
All you own feeds me bright certainty:
Cacti, gleaming gold, a lone bird's coo.

What sights of you have snow and fiddle spun—
Flapping flags of shining cities too?
Those shrieks of boys at play—were they from you?
Are you dying with the sinking sun?

I roam through typhoons, crystal ocean's blue;
Perhaps a stray scent there brings you to light?
And all through black and silver alleys, true,

With sobs of woe or laughs of glad delight,
Yes, every day I go in search of you:
Toward you still roams the crimson path of night.

ISLAND AT NIGHT

Frauenwörth

The lake flows slowly toward the distant land.
Perhaps (somewhere, somehow) it finds that land.
The pallid banks cry out their desolation.
(Reed beds carry so much desolation.)

The meadow's grown all bloomless now and bare.
The huts now stand completely empty, bare.
Belated birds have sought a long, long rest.
The final moth has found its own dark rest.

A giant shadow will loom here at the end,
With morning nearly forgotten at the end.
Still, a slim white birch will hang at evening,
A white nun still pray in the evening.

ADVENTURE

I've lost the way; I'm miles from everything.
Beginning, middle, end—all fled from me!
I feel I'm borne inside a deep, deep ring;
I hear my soft steps echo quietly
Far off in some unknown and foreign land;
I hear my mild words drift down through the spaces
Of a stillness dark on every hand.
I stride my way through many strange, strange places
And feel I halt, in silence, as at home
Yet must go on (*as if forever, I must go*)
And smiling, hoping to return, I roam . . .
I know the room—already, this I know:
The bluish lamp of a sweetly-silenced light.
I heard this voice a thousand years ago,
Her trembling welcome in the night.

ODE TO SEBASTIAN

Oh, you were a tree! Inside you birds were sleeping.
Winds wedded beautifully. Leopards coolly inclined.
A lamb—a cloud—lay lightly bedded on you.
And you were vast! The shadows of your boughs
Arched over the roofs of all the most distant cities.
Yes, you were vast! I could not elude your roots,
Like playful hands that tightly twined around
A ball; my ankles sank and bled with tears.
And you were huge! And Venus clung to you
And faded—upset—when you spoke with storms;
You bore the sun on your uplifted head;
Night sank in sorrow when you bowed down low.

MOUTH

I am now no more than a mouth that speaks to you—
Now all the rest of me has slipped from view—
My face, my body, and all I'd gathered to me.
Yes, now no more than a stammering mouth, you see,
That's kept on living—to herald to you its death:
It's open and now must fill you with its breath.

A CHILDHOOD PRAYER

At night there is a dark black hound, Lord Jesus:
He comes clawing down the wooden stair.
A whitish shadow now and then, Lord Jesus,
Stands on the meadow's fringe in the morning air.
Savior, the bloom I've sown for you with care
Now rises ever higher toward your glow.
You draw her close. I'll be a shepherd so
The little lambs and I will be as one.
Now all the chicks have hatched, but one is lame.
Your candle before her, Mother said each flame
Will flow to find its way to your great sun.

from ROBINSON (1923-24)

THE JOURNEY

The vessel bore him on. His glad lips sang
Of water, wind, vast spaces in his mind:
"Far places! Flight! Desire's fast-fading pang!
And eyes—o eyes—still much too blind;
O breath, which never drinks quite deep enough;
O breast that never bursts; heart's heated core
That can't quite fade to sparks that wind could snuff;
O voice, o never wholly-melted ore,
I bear you forth to fresh new lands of dawn,
A homeland ever soaked in sun and strange!"

Or so he thought as waves propelled him on
From rock to rock—yes, thought despite each change.
The moon loomed like a girl he might embrace . . .
Then he fell overboard. The sea slid from him, wave
On wave. He lay quite still: a slim white trace
In seaweed, sand—as in his grave.

ROBINSON FINDS HIMSELF ON THE ISLAND BEACH

And this was all he found when he woke: the sight
Of a body lying in agony in the sand.
Before him flowed a sea in hyacinth night,
Behind, in broken blues, an endless land.

The wind ran fast; the sharp-beaked seagulls poked
Around for prey; and husky monkeys screamed
While huge red moths stirred whirring wings and stroked
His flesh in a feverish frenzy as they dreamed.

He lay in pain, a body swathed in fire.
In love he raised his hand up high.
The roar of the world all round cried like a choir
And said with strict and limiting knowledge: *I.*

ROBINSON SETTLES ON THE ISLAND'S EDGE

So then it was—with that word—that he began
The long discourse with himself: for he
Was all alone. And he was merely a man—
A little island in the great big sea.
Escape plots failed. No outside answer came.

Yet longing ever remained in him. To trade
The barren strand for the lush grapevines and game
Of the rich inland? A deal he could not have made.
For the sea's murmuring meant hope. So he waxed on the rim
Of earth and water and himself. It meant
That dialogues commenced to take place in him,
A thin-stretched wall through which the voices went.

ROBINSON MAKES A STOOL

I teach a tough task to my unskilled hands,
Which don't know anything. My mouth's grown mute,
As if my memory'd melted in time's sands.

I've built a thing lame, crooked . . . Destitute.
And now I have to train my tongue to say,
With childlike and astonished timbre, *"Chair."*

My numb but thrilled hands praise themselves today
For their first creation. Results of right action there:
I sit. (That's almost as it was for me
One time before, early on: I bent my knee.)

ROBINSON DANCES

And now I greet you, God, in all the glow
Of early morning: freed, I rise and swing
Right up in dance like a whole wide world and know
I'm one with you. And then I fling
Both grief, joy down like rotted clothes. Of all
My bound-up being, naught remains. The weight
Has dropped from arms and feet; I rise, I fall
In empty space; I thrust on through; and light
Breaks through me, I through light: a radiance
Wherein I burst, o Lord. *Am* I? Am I *not?*

For you I dance the boundless dance.

ROBINSON FEEDS HIS LAMB

I find no cities here that cry out: "Build!"
No wine enticing me to come and swill.
No foolish wish to have my lust fulfilled
By some strange dame; no deed that needs good will.

Here, out of me, and sought by me, I've met
The Real once more diffused, more crystallized,
More *island*-like—a clear framework and yet
Too pure for clean deceit by the non-sacralized:

(Fond lie: He took a wicker cage and set
A lamb in it he tended, fed, and prized.)

ROBINSON IS TIRED

Now I will just fall down—fall like a stone
Somebody's thrown, and with a lusty groan
Sink into the deep, deep grass as daylight glides
Right into night's unbeing. In me abides
A lust for oblivion: to be aware—
Awake—is sapping as sickness, and the white
Plague of knowledge has already bloomed in my hair.
Sleep, rinse me darkly pure! Let me lie in night;
Let Robinson rest like hills, his bearing birth
Of mere deep shadows: dark thing of Earth.

ROBINSON AND THE PARROT

That time my arrow struck you and you fell—
You lovely color-play of blue and green—
You healed quite slowly. When your wings were well,
You still had no desire to flee the scene:
I often heard you flutter on some bough,
Your voice, by now, a quite familiar one
That, mocking, called me back no matter how
I tried to flee. *O Robinson!*

THE DEMONS SEIZE ROBINSON

Could I have lived here for so long that there
Is nothing here that's strange to me? A tree
Whose trunk is veiled by mist and wind-torn hair—
I ran into it once—have things gone bad for me
Between the shoulders since then? A toad there was,
All spotted, fat . . . Slurped up by the snake, just so.
And then a limb lay shamelessly obvious
On a swamp. A stone perhaps; but then, as though
Torn out of me. And too: a river split
As through my heart so painfully. . . Oh,
Decay now opens up in me. I saw it—
In violet—a measured yellow glow.
The South bears off my brain. I'm swept apart
From myself; my end I no longer know.
All happens in me. *Is* me. I'm at the heart.

ROBINSON FINDS FRIDAY

He stopped when he saw me, his fright-filled eyes immense.
When I saw *him*, I stood as if turned to stone,
Mid-stride. O heavenly offense!
O well-shaped man! O joy, to be overthrown
By love of the kindred sight of lips and eyes
And knees and hands and ears and five-toed feet
Like mine . . . This quite familiar form just shies
A bit, then spreads its feet, makes no retreat:
An answer to my call. Sweet melody
Of the human voice! Do I share such pulchritude?
Has God created this playmate for me
Simply to mirror my solitude?

ROBINSON WALKS ALONG THE RIM OF HIS ENCLOSURE

Is there another who knows when his time has ended?
Did he, like me, find himself ever hemmed in again?
This is the fence of a land that has been well-tended.
My life has settled down here in this pen
Like a flock of birds, a day for every stake,
And they were lined up over many a year.
Strange transformation! Out of the loathsome ache
Of senseless drudgery, I've found some cheer
At last. As if to make that burden more
Understandable . . . Some cheer, I yet insist.
As if this fence might someday stand before
Inquiring minds to prove I did exist.

ROBINSON SAYS FAREWELL TO HIS ISLAND

And now you teach me the final thing: to go.
O tough farewell, my little island—land
Who taught me, brought me up. I kiss your strand.
To live and bed down here, I still yearn so
To do! For we'd grown one through long, long love:
My soul prowled, thundering, through your woods and plunged,
Roaring, into your streams; my heart, too, lunged
Up into my throat; I scanned the sky above
And sang in words from deep in me: "O state
Bestowed on me, in deep kinship, to serve!
O body of earth and water, salt and slate!"
And now a pallid twilight-tempering of nerve,
A withering of will . . . No! Let there be
For us—transformed—no lingering,
And but a slender strait, eternity,
Within that track of endless traveling!

from IMAGO (1922-29)

JUST OPEN . . .

Just open up the door;
Just step onto the sill;
Just lift your eyes a bit more
And feel the bright rays spill
In vast and gleaming streams
That, like the fields, now flow
And dance in heavy dreams
That rise and glimmer, glow . . .
No softly-surging thrill
(wind-borne) you're not meant for:
Just step onto the sill;
Just open up the door!

CACTI

For years on end, out of sound, in pots, they brood:
Strange birds in love with themselves and obstinate
Within a grim, mysterious servitude
To form: they're crosses, bowls, and cones, a bit

Reminiscent of misshapen heads, perhaps a pear,
Or even a ghost made of stone, a snake, a hand;
And so estranged that, like great shocks of hair,
Their spines define their world-defying stand

Behind anarchic poses, hour on hour
As god and prophet in witness, self-possessed *I*
Till—all of a sudden—silent, flowing in flower,
They hide, they immolate themselves, they die.

BALLAD OF THE NAMELESS ONE

He lived because he'd been born. So there!
He found no other reason.
Quite early, his mother loved his hair.
One loved his mouth for a season
But thought it a trifle so told him bye
Before he had time to shed tears.
And all of it was such small fry
That by the time he'd started to die
He'd forgotten about it for years.

TO MY FATHER

Quite early, you dipped the morning gardens' steam
Deep into my soul. You gave a kindred name—
Blue sickle—to the moon. The animals,
O wizard, followed you obediently;
You conjured up strange flowers in the evenings
Between the ferns and stones. And once me too.
And you go on the same strange ways you did
Back then. Already you know the shimmer of
White hair. So you go on, forever knowing
The infinite first, and death as once the flowers,
The dew. Yet love drifts on, a dark stretch of water
Far and endlessly traveled by each alone.
Heralding help, the barque that bore you never
Washed me aside; my cry for you did not
Ever reach you in the land of night; I sink,
You shine—one last solace, perhaps—transfigured as star.

CARNIVAL OF THE UNELATED

I'd run away, escaped scot-free
(Was dancing strangely, in a strange land);
Already they wished to christen me
(One even had a name on hand);

He called me what they'd called me way
Back then, a long, long time before . . .
And then I knew that even today,
Beneath the painted dress I wore,

They recognized the one now left—
One hardly known to herself at all:
Her heart cast out, she stood bereft
Of love, face flushed, backed to the wall.

A PROPHET'S YOUTH

I loved linens and stretched my hands with joy
Toward gentle silks. *He* whispered:
"A stag's hard hide will clothe *you*, boy."

I sat at table and couldn't help but stare
At the golden wine. He said to me, loud and clear:
"The bitter root, my friend, will be *your* fare."

Life in the castle was hard. But when I fled
My way to the highest crenellation, he called:
"O what a good sleep, thorn and stone your bed!"

I lay with a lass, and, cradled at her breast,
I dreamed the dream of home. He already knew
I'd roam alone and cursed, with never a rest.

So I broke down. Because I believed what he said,
His sure and invincible knowledge conquered me.
His smile loomed great above my head.

DON QUIXOTE STRUGGLES WITH GOD

When you should bless me, what does it avail,
Colossal one, that you should lash and flail
Me; that your power, blesséd one, should fail
Me; that your breath, angry one, should leave me pale?

Now I'm lying somewhere. And I'm little more
Than dust in the dust past recognition, poor
And small. And your great eye wanders o'er
This desert spot where I've been cast ashore.

I'll not forsake you, though, because, when you
Deny me other struggles, Pure One, heed:
I'll call you up in puddles mirroring you;

I'll fight with you, my only foe; and when
The dust chokes me, you do. With each deep need,
I seize you, Lord. You bless me then.

THE HERMIT

For years he no longer had scattered seed,
And yet the grain still ripened for him;
At last he left the oats on the stem
And let his horse go free on the mead.

He once broke berries from a bush
Whenever he had a stomach to still
But then forewent this to fulfill
His soul's need for a deeper hush.

He sat by his hut both day and night;
The hut collapsed in wind and rain;
Soon hopes of seeing his legs were vain,
The grass had grown to such a height.

It slowly twined up through his hand;
Sans out or in, he seemed a sieve;
Resisting resistance, he could but give
Himself up to the years like sand.

THE PROCESSION OF THE ANIMALS

Before the clueless beasts could say how or why,
They found themselves surrounded, wall to wall.
And yet quite far away in the boundless sky,
A train still moves, as livid as a pall.

One night the moon was in their reveries.
Drawn into, borne by its pallid light, they broke down.
As if they were climbing into thickly-leaved trees,
They climbed inside the cathedral's woven crown.

In dream they climbed until they reached the last
Gable's branches and were hardly awake
When their feet came to rest in the void, held fast
Within a space they could not escape or mistake

For heaven, still less the earth. And now they were quite
Without a home. They stared into that zone
Of blinding light till left forlorn in night.
And then, their faces crazed, they turned to stone.

UNENDING SPRING

A fragment

I see you rise in the boughs again, o spring. I heed
How the withered branches, in your soft wrath,
Now grow and bloom again, see the meadow's path
Rise up the mountain beneath it, scatter like seed.

Then you'll spread snow round the peaks once more—a snow
That fades; o whiteness ordained once more to go
Away, stream down the vale; o loneliness,
Dissolved, flowing far, with a wild sort of tenderness.

AN EVENING IN EARLY AUTUMN

It spreads out far and wide, the spacious land.
The sky still laves the mountain peaks in light,
Yet from one side, it calmly lifts a hand
To its face to make the darkling mask of night.

Fat lambs are grazing on the meadow grass.
The gardens teem with herbs in rich quantity.
Like tracks of gold, the woods of autumn pass;
Firm fruit gleams in its rind upon the tree.

It is the very last of these brief days.
All things stand ripe and round and silent there,
Adrift, bewitched, and poised on scales that raise
Both life and death aloft in thinnest air.

SNOW

Heaven's tears: Rain fell today
As lethally as all end of mirth
Upon our dear demolished play,
Upon the decaying earth.

Autumn's already hurled her down
In wanton crimson ruin and wrong;
Gently she rocks in her shattered crown,
Humming her odd and forlorn song.

Yet there, in those silver flashes of frost,
See: rigidity's fall.
Blessèd form: the no-longer lost
World dances, in crystal, redemption for all.

YEAR'S END

Decrepit year! You rush, with mounting zest,
On toward your end, desiring your last rest
In deep and boundless realms that house the dead.
Yet see: I rush more quickly—toward the red
Of fresh new dawns with greed, ahead of you.
Do come! Fly past! Blow out your flue!
Accursed, bogged down, smeared with the stain
Of great fatigue, adorned with hurt and pain . . .
Pass on! *I* will! Yes, die: I can and may
Arise again, o pure and clear new day!

I LOOKED AT YOU

I looked at you and wish I might
Have never seen you: I've grown wild;
You're huge and lead me, slight of sight,
A crazy child.

Where once firm walls stood all about
Me (sure, if wind-swept, they would stand),
I can't hide now; I'm driven out,
In no man's land.

And, wherever I might be,
Hemlock flourishes, sweet with fear,
Breathes heavily, speaks painfully
Of your lips, my dear.

Whatever turn or path I take,
My dreams oppress me; my dim soul
And body, helpless, cannot break
Your dark control.

ANCIENT . . .

Be calm, my love. Your lips to mine,
We aged as we never dreamed we could.
In one never-stilled bond, we grew tall and fine
And old as the ancient wood.

Old as the moon, my face of light;
And you, slender scythe, for ages, you
Have stood erect in heaven's night
Reaping me ever anew.

From the old, dark seed, old as the sea,
It rises in ripened and fiery flood
Between us, through eternity:
The dark, eternal blood.

ON A PACKET OF LETTERS

I picked it up (the faded thing that I
Had long declared deceased) as gingerly
As an ash-filled urn, concerned the dust might fly
When I carried it. Yet still, it burdened me:

Now vanished heavens crashed down shining, streaming;
Temptation, like the serpent once, lisped now;
And long-lost hells returned now, beaming,
Nestling snugly round my cheeks and brow.

And then I watched the flowering flames ascend
The way life burns—hot, livid, naked, red—
And speak, Greek-chorus-like: this now is the end.
We live, we live. But you are dead.

SONNET

Avert your gaze! It struck me hard and stayed
To strike me fatally. Do know I fade not quite
Against my will, nor slip away afraid;
Just take, from my death, this strange dark light;
Take your look away! No thicket stands
Prepared for me as for the wounded deer
Who soon will meet his end; no craft commands
Me yet to hide and watch and wait in fear . . .
So be merciful! And, doing so, annul
For me this hideous scene from history,
This curious image shown to the imperial
Strolling Nero for his scrutiny:
A face impaled on a stake, waxing slack and dull;
He studied its agony long and smilingly.

CERTAINTY

Be patient! Take it all in stride
As each day's chains just glide on past.
The start (which can't be grasped, descried)
Won't end. And will grow vast.
The middle? (Aimless, more open, narrow . . .)
Let her waver, let her roam:
At last a stricter, harsher harrow
Will intervene to send you home.

AFTERWORD: THE FATE OF A POET

In the case of gifted poets who die quite young, perhaps it is idle to speculate as to what they might have done had more time been granted to them. And yet such speculation is only natural; our grief dictates it. So it was when Maria Luise Weissmann died, quite suddenly and unexpectedly, of heart failure at the age of thirty: her peers on the German literary scene were shocked by what they considered a wasteful and wholly unjust death. Gottfried Kölwel described the power behind her early demise as "the darkness that no one has fathomed yet" (VII), while Otto Heuschel compared his distress to the grief he had felt on the passing of Hugo von Hofmannsthal (XII).

Yet though he, like others, wished to cry out against the "senselessness of fate" (XII), to do so would be a "fruitless bother," he argued; instead, he felt that it would be far better to preserve her memory in the souls of those left behind (XII-XIII). And indeed, this is what other friends and associates of Weissmann set out to do, and succeeded in doing; for affirmed in their memorials and testaments is a sense of Weissmann's significance as a poet of great genius and promise, a sense of the importance—even the sacredness—of poetry for the writers of this time, as well as a sense that poetry outlasts death. "There are no dead things lying here before me," Heuschele says of the letters and essays that Weissmann had recently sent him, photos of her that he had at hand, but most of all, her books—all of which he refers to as "relics" (XIII). Even if "ripeness and perfection had not yet been reached," he asserts, the work that she had accomplished in ten years' time points toward them (XIV).

Heuschele stresses the influence of Hofmannsthal and Rilke (XIV) on her work, which Wilhelm von Schramm (Dimpfl 9) and Paul Alverdes (14) affirm. "[T]his early-silenced mouth may have learned suppleness and the art of pleasant sounds from Hofmannsthal and above all from Rilke," Alverdes states (14); and one is inclined to agree that, of her predecessors, perhaps the voice and manner of Rilke seems strongest. Her musings on cacti are in the vein of Rilke's *Dinggedichte*, while "The Carousel" takes its subject from Rilke's poem of the same name, though Weissmann's treatment differs in that she focuses on the way a child eager for diversion appears to launch the carousel animals into

56

motion, and a detailed comparison of the two might not be fair given that Rilke's piece is fifteen lines longer. Yet "The Gorilla," which Weissmann no doubt would not have written had she not known of Rilke's "The Panther," offers dimensions that the former does not. Though each describes the plight of a caged beast in a zoo, and though each uses the suitably confined form of the sonnet to do so, Weissmann's gorilla rails against his condition in a way that is almost human and so connects us more fully to a species closer to our own, admittedly, than Rilke's panther. Weissmann's sympathy with her subject reaches a climax in her tenth line, when she abruptly truncates her iambic pentameter and in so doing suggests the way that the frustrated beast suddenly, surprisingly launches into a cry of protest at his entrapment. Thus, even though Weissmann's gorilla, like Rilke's panther, tends to roam his cell in a daze, his occasional heroic defiance distinguishes him from that other victim.

To be sure, Weissmann's literary contemporaries could see early on that she was no mere imitator of Hofmannsthal and Rilke, but an original voice in her own right. Heuschele, in particular, is struck by her "intimate and early contact with death," which "seems to have belonged to her life" (XIV). He goes on to cite features distinctive to her: her poems are very "tender and silent, intimate but not soft; they are so strong that they pierce us deeply" (XIV). We do not find in Weissmann's poetry, he contends, "that which moves our time with its loud and unrefined superficiality" (XV). On the other hand, the "most peculiar and typical feature that gives these verses their dark gleam" is their "mythic," "timeless," "powerfully-primal" quality (X). This forms "the darkly-glowing subsoil of the Robinson poems"; it shows in the last poems, such as the especially profound "Auszug der Tiere" ("Procession of the Animals").

Like Heuschele, Paul Alverdes finds in Weissmann a poet who clearly rises above the mood of her day. He begins his memorial to her by quoting Goethe: "Humans are productive in poetry and art only so long as they are religious; otherwise they just become imitative and repetitive" (13). He then goes on to call that quotation prophetic, as well as a "key to the whole artistic misery of our time":

Presumably more than ever is being written, rhymed, and painted, but presumably it has never been easier to call oneself an artist. It is shocking to think of what is put forward to us as art . . . [U]nreligious or matter-or-fact or quite trivial, . . . it remains from the outset external and beneath the actually productive or creative, that is to say, religious sphere. (13)

He argues that, while Weissmann was indeed a "faithless and unchristian person, who, as she made known, avoided church," her poetry constitutes "one of the few truly religious, truly soulful manifestations of the younger German literature, and the loss that we have suffered . . . shakes us as only the loss of a-too-soon-extinguished genius can" (13).

To illuminate wherein her religiosity resides, Alverdes cites a quotation from her autobiographical sketch "Kleines impromptu im Herbst":

> I am a lonely human being and a pagan . . . I could never kneel down and pray, worshipping without wish. The thing that intoxicates me is the thing that I seek to accompany me, so my loneliness can be eased in love. I wish to be that which enflames me. (*Gesammelte Dichtungen* 112)

As one instance of an individual's union with that which intoxicates or enflames him, Alverdes cites a passage from "Die Dämonen fassen Robinson" ("The Demons Seize Robinson"): "All happens in me. *Is* me. I'm at the heart," Robinson exclaims when the demons grip him (13).

The achievement of such a union, Alverdes affirms, lies at the center of what he refers to as Weissmann's "Natur Religiösitat" or natural piety:

> This human being knows no difference between herself and nature, which surrounds her, or will know none. She will include herself in the perhaps awful and riddlesome, yet infinite and immortal, connection that she is still aware of there; she wants it with surrender of herself, if it must be; with relinquishment and decay of body and person; but she does not want to differentiate herself. For to do so would be to be without God and . . . without even nature: an unbearable,

horrifying thought of only senseless loneliness and isolation . . .
Her longing is for transformation, not for staying the same; it is
return, fading, death. (13-14)

As evidence for this longing, Alverdes cites "Robinson ist Müde"
("Robinson is Tired"):

> In me abides
> A lust for oblivion: to be aware,
> Awake is sapping as sickness, and the white
> Plague of knowledge has already bloomed in my hair.
> Sleep, rinse me darkly pure! Let me lie in night;
> Let Robinson rest like hills, his bearing birth
> Of mere deep shadows: dark thing of Earth.

Because of this restless yearning, Alverdes argues, Weissmann's poems
"lack almost totally the festive or directly celebratory and praising"
(14). One could cite exceptions, such as "Nur öffne die Tür" ("Just
open the Door") and "Schnee" ("Snow"). Yet if we consider her work
as a whole— notably the Robinson sequence, the responses to the
natural world, and the love poems—we are no doubt inclined to agree
with Alverdes' conclusions regarding the questing nature of her poetic
soul:

> Even the reflections on the beloved, a kiss or an embrace,
> appear . . . the signs of an eternally transforming, restless, and
> Self-seeking existence, and each movement of the heart and
> tender breath of the lips moves the breathing form along with
> it. Also, the landscape that she speaks of in her best verses is
> marked by a boundlessness, stimulated by death, and symbolic
> not of a present life--of life in the here and now—but of
> transience and eternal return. (14)

Her profound longing, as poet—her ceaseless *Sehnsucht* or yearning—
places her firmly within the German Romantic tradition, and one might
be inclined to wonder whether something in her life imbued her with
this quality. Yet the facts as they are give few clues, so we may assume
that it was merely an aspect—and an essential one—of her poetic
temperament. She led, as Monika Dimpfl has noted, an "industrious
and lovely childhood directed early on toward things of the mind" (3).

Her father, a teacher, encouraged her intellectually. The family did move quite often: Dr. Karl Weissmann was transferred from Schweinfurt am Main, where she was born, to Hof in Oberfranken when she was ten (3), then from Hof to Nuremberg when she was fourteen. Dimpfl regards the three years she spent in Nuremberg as decisive ones, years during which her "future relationships to poetry, love, and religion were determined" (5). In Nuremberg, she began to write stories and poems; and, by her nineteenth year, she was already seeing her work published (under the pseudonym "Hermann Wels") in the *Fränkische Kurier* (6). Her appointment as secretary of Nuremberg's literary society in that same year led to her meeting the poet and publisher Heinrich F. S. Bachmair at a reading he gave there. The two immediately fell in love. Few letters between the two are accessible, Dimpfl states, and we have mainly only the highly subjective memories of her cousin Wilhelm von Schramm to form a picture of the two lovers at this time (8). Schramm himself, who was off at war for some of this period, seems to have vied for his cousin's attentions, the two sharing an interest in the new literature: Reinhard Göring's *Seeschlacht,* which begins with a scream no doubt inspired by Edvard Munch's painting, as well as works by Klabund and, "naturally, Rilke" (Dimpfl 9).

Maria was, in her cousin's words, "slender, delicate, and sensitive," with "whitish-blond hair" (Dimpfl 7), whereas Bachmair's was "an ugly, yet fascinating face with its jutting chin and overly-large, ever lightly-veiled eyes" (Dimpfl 9). She called him Sebastian, after the martyr whose name he had given himself (Dimpfl 7); and her nickname explains the title of one of the poems in *Das frühe Fest.* "I was jealous," recalled Schramm, who found it hard to believe that his cousin had been proposed to so quickly, and by such a distinguished man (Dimpfl 9). "[H]e can recite brilliantly," Maria had reported to him; evidently, one midnight in the literary café in Nuremberg, Bachmair had intoned Rilke's "Der Knabe," and Schramm claims this as having been the moment when she decided to marry Bachmair (10). Whatever the case, the couple did not wed until June of 1922, the year Bachmair was appointed production director for Musarion Verlag (11).

In the years that intervened, Bachmair's movements are easier to trace than Weissmann's are, but they also shed light on the historical context to her career. In January 1919, he formed his second press, and, with

Leo Scherpenbach, established the bookstore "Die Bücherkiste" in Munich, along with a monthly journal in March 1919 under the same name (9). Then, on April 15, 1919, the playwright Ernst Toller appointed him Commander of the Red Artillery in Dachau. On May 1 of that year, following the retreat of the Red Army and the collapse of the Räterepublik, Bachmair fled from Munich to Franconia, surfacing momentarily in Nuremberg. From there he hastened on, by bicycle, until, on the 14th of June, he wrote to Maria to say he had been arrested in Rothenburg ob der Tauber and was now in police custody:

> But rest assured: it won't be bad. Those whom Leviné (whose name is on the wall above my Strohsack), gladly knew to be living multiply more and more each day. (Dimpfl 12)

As Dimpfl notes, Weissman's poem "June 1919" is set during this month. Though it makes no allusion to Bachmair's situation, its mood is one of tense and brooding expectancy:

> The dark dawn bore me, heavy, in her womb
> And for the pale morning, dying, brought me to be,
> I who with the wild roses slowly bloom.
> The hills must lend their cool blue shade to me
> When midday hurts me with its sharp, steep glow.
> The slim plank swaying over the brook below
> Leads on toward dusk with tired and timid tread.
> The bare walls silently cave in at night;
> The black woods stride their way about my bed.

Bachmair was found guilty of high treason for lending financial assistance to the Red Army cause and sentenced to one and one half years of imprisonment, first at Lichtenau bei Ansbach, then at Niederschönenfeld bei Donauwörth (Dimpfl 13). After his release in 1920, Maria joined him in Pasing. Up until then, she assisted her cousin Wilhelm at Bachmair's bookstore and also worked for the society for Buddhist Living and the publisher Oskar Schloß (14-15). Though her poems make no direct reference to world events, and, though she was certainly not as active politically as Bachmair was, she did participate for a time in 1919 in the short-lived revolutionary literary society "Das Junge Franken," whose initiator was Alexander Abusch, a young

Communist who after 1945 went on to serve as a high-level cultural functionary in the German Democratic Republic (Dimpfl 15).

Meanwhile, Weissmann continued to write. Her subjects were wide-ranging—saints, prophets, animals wild and domestic, characters from classic literature such as Don Quixote and Robinson Crusoe, the modern city, dreamscapes, death, nature, and love—and her treatment of them was, by turns, solemn, witty, whimsical, and profound, often even within the same poem. Like her 19th-century predecessors, the German Romantics, Weissmann demonstrates a love of nature, but she is especially sensitive to its frailty in our modern age, as well as to the frailty of human beings, and in ways that make her particularly relevant for today. "The Strange City," for instance, shows the precariousness of human life in the modern urban world:

> I shove myself at gates rammed shut, locked fast;
> I stare at myriad masks of fright all round;
> I'm tired—so tired—yet cannot go to sleep.

Here, Weissmann's readiness to confront this world clearly links her to the earlier, Berlin-based Georg Heym, but her voice is arguably more anxiously personal. She has the courage to expose her vulnerability, and this fact makes her a braver poet in some ways, I would contend, than the two early-twentieth-century German-language poets best-known to English audiences, Rilke and Trakl. "The Gorilla" I have already discussed, but others also suggest her distinctiveness. Yes, while "Abend in Früh-Herbst" ("Evening in Early Autumn") recalls Trakl in the way it traces the imperceptible change of the seasons, how often is Trakl (or Rilke) so directly, personally emotional as Weissmann is in the following poem about the coming of spring?

> Just open up the door;
> Just step onto the sill;
> Just lift your eyes a bit more
> And feel the bright rays spill
> In vast and gleaming streams
> That, like the fields, now flow
> And dance in heavy dreams
> That rise and glimmer and glow . . .
> No softly-surging thrill

(wind-borne) you're not meant for:
Just step onto the sill;
Just open up the door!

In her treatment of love, as well, she exhibits a candor that is disarming yet also daring. "Ich Sah Dich An" ("I Looked at you") and "Sonett" ("Sonnet") are cases in point, these lines from the latter being especially indicative:

Avert your gaze! It struck me hard and stayed
To strike me fatally. Do know I fade not quite
Against my will, nor slip away afraid;
Just take, from my death, this strange dark light;
Take your look away!

Her willingness to bare her feelings so openly links her to her American contemporary Edna St. Vincent Millay, who also couched her intense feelings in the stately attire of the sonnet and other fixed forms, though Weissmann is not as apt to depend on inversion of syntax as Millay is. A more extended study might show where she stands among her female German-language contemporaries; and as a way of inciting such a discussion, one might pose that, while she shares with the now more well-known Mascha Kaléko, for one, a certain frivolity at times, she is less *confined* to the realm of the purely personal and more inclined to venture into the minds and hearts of characters outside herself (a prophet, a saint, Don Quixote, Robinson Crusoe), the result being a timeless (or as Heuschele said, *mythic*) treatment of universal human themes. Discussing her archetypally-grounded "Abenteuer" ("Adventure") in light of Kaléko's moving yet still highly personal and historically-specific "Im Exil" ("In Exile") might offer a case in point.

Whether comparisons with poets who lived longer, and whose treatments of subjects differs from hers, is fair or not, the fact remains that Weissmann's output during her brief career was prodigious. And her work also found favor with several influential literary figures, including those already mentioned but also Georg Britting, who published four of her early poems in the journal *Die Sichel.* Yet the going was tough, even so; Britting's efforts to place her first book were fruitless (Dimpfl 16-17). After she herself went on to send that collection to several publishers, the entire process of having her work handled by so many strangers proved so chilling to her that she determined to buy a fur with the money that she would receive from the sale of the book, a fur that would not be "like a corpse, with a flat muzzle and many tails," but a "a great dark fur" that she would wrap around her and dwell within "as in a dark cave: I am a lonely beast that has no hiding place other than itself" (Dimpfl 17).

Finally, in 1922, the year she and Bachmair married, he also published her first book, *Das frühe Fest*. Now editor of the *Bayerischer Arbeiter-Zeitung*, Abusch, with a hint of mockery, referred to them as poems of "charming lyrical and girlish beauty" and noted what a contradiction it was for Weissmann to have gone so far left in her thought as to have been torn away from her bourgeois family into the arms of the Räterepublikaner (Dimpfl 17-18).

Despite such mixed reviews as this, Weissmann kept writing. More books followed: *Robinson,* in an edition of 180 copies in handmade paper with deckle edges (Dimpfl 17) and dedicated to her father; *Mit einer Sammlung von Kakteen* in 1926; then her translations of Verlaine in 1927. Still, there would be no hint in her work of the turbulence of the time. Weissmann died in 1929 at the age of 30, four years before Hitler came into power. The Third Reich would not endure; nor would Communism in Europe. Capitalism clambers on with its characteristic rises and falls. Weissmann's poems remain, in a realm outside the noise of history, profound and sublime.

WORKS CITED

Alverdes, Paul. "Maria Luise Weissmann." *Der Kunstwart: Monatshefte für Kunst, Literatur, und Leben.* Heft #1, 44. Jahrgang. October 1930. 13-15. Print.

Bachmair, Heinrich F. S. "Nachwort des Herausgebers." ("Publisher's Afterword.") In *Imago: Ausgewählte Gedichte* of Maria Luise Weissmann. Starnberg am See: Heinrich F. S. Bachmair, 1946. Print.

Barnstone, Willis. "On the Translation of *Sonnets to Orpheus.*" In *Sonnets to Orpheus* by Rainer Maria Rilke. Trans. Willis Barnstone. Boston: Shambala Publications, Inc., 2004. Print.

Dimpfl, Monika. *"Ich bin ein einsamer Mensch und ein Heide. . .": Die Dichterin Maria Luise Weissmann.* München: Bayerischer Rundfunk, 1991. Print.

Heuschele, Otto. "In Memoriam." In *Maria Luise Weissmann: Zum Gedächtnis.* Pasing bei München: Heinrich F. S. Bachmair, 1932. XII-XVI. Print.

Kölwel, Gottfried. "Gedächtnisrede." ("Commemorative Speech.") In *Maria Luise Weissmann: Zum Gedächtnis.* Pasing bei München: Heinrich F. S. Bachmair, 1932. VII-XI. Print.

Weissmann, Maria Luise. "Kleines impromptu im Herbst." In *Gesammelte Dichtungen.* Pasing bei München: Heinrich F. S. Bachmair, 1932. 111-114. Print.

ABOUT THE TRANSLATOR

William Ruleman's previous books include two collections of his own poems (*A Palpable Presence* and *Sacred and Profane Loves*, both from Feather Books), as well as translations of poems from Rilke's *Neue Gedichte* (WillHall Books, 2003), of Stefan Zweig's fiction in *Vienna Spring: Early Novellas and Stories* (Ariadne Press, 2010), of prose and poems by Zweig in *A Girl and the Weather* (Cedar Springs Books, 2014), and of poems by the German Romantics in *Verse for the Journey: Poems on the Wandering Life* (also from Cedar Springs Books). He is currently Professor of English at Tennessee Wesleyan College.